# A Note to Parents

DK READERS is a compelling program for beginning readers, designed in conjunction with leading literacy experts, including Dr. Linda Gambrell, Distinguished Professor of Education at Clemson University. Dr. Gambrell has served as President of the National Reading Conference, the College Reading Association, and the International Reading Association.

Beautiful illustrations and superb full-color photographs combine with engaging, easy-to-read stories to offer a fresh approach to each subject in the series. Each DK READER is guaranteed to capture a child's interest while developing his or her reading skills, general knowledge, and love of reading.

The five levels of DK READERS are aimed at different reading abilities, enabling you to choose the books that are exactly right for your child:

**Pre-level 1**: Learning to read
**Level 1**: Beginning to read
**Level 2**: Beginning to read alone
**Level 3**: Reading alone
**Level 4**: Proficient readers

The "normal" age at which a child begins to read can be anywhere from three to eight years old. Adult participation through the lower levels is very helpful for providing encouragement, discussing storylines, and sounding out unfamiliar words.

No matter which level you select, you can be sure that you are helping your child learn to read, then read to learn!

**DK LONDON**
Series Editor Deborah Lock
Project Editor Camilla Gersh
US Senior Editor Shannon Beatty
Art Director Martin Wilson
Producer, Pre-production
Francesca Wardell
Jacket Designer Martin Wilson

**DK DELHI**
Editor Nandini Gupta
Art Editor Jyotsna Julka
DTP Designers
Anita Yadav, Syed Md Farhan
Picture Researcher Deepak Negi
Deputy Managing Editor
Soma B. Chowdhury

Reading Consultant
Linda Gambrell, Ph.D.

Subject Consultants
Dr. Victoria Ogilvy and Sam Taylor, Froglife

First American Edition, 2014
Published in the United States by DK Publishing
345 Hudson Street, New York, New York 10014

The publisher would like to thank the following for
their kind permission to reproduce their photographs:
(Key: a=above, b=below/bottom, c=center, l=left, r=right, t=top)
1 Corbis: David A. Northcott (br). 3 Fotolia: Anyka (c). 4 Corbis: Jared Hobbs /
All Canada Photos (bl). Dreamstime.com: Amwu (cl). 4–5 Dreamstime.com:
Michelle Milliman (b). 5 Dreamstime.com: Isselee (cr). 6 Dorling Kindersley:
Jan Van Der Voort (c). 7 Alamy Images: David Cook / blueshiftstudios (bl);
LOOK Die Bildagentur der Fotografen GmbH (c); Woodystock (bc, br).
8 Alamy Images: Herbert Kehrer / imagebroker (br). 9 Alamy Images: Redmond
O. Durrell (bl); Sean Bolton (tr). Dreamstime.com: Isselee (br).
10 Alamy Images: Marvin Dembinsky Photo Associates (c). 11 Alamy Images:
Joel Sartore / National Geographic Image Collection (bc, br); Life on white (bl).
12 Science Photo Library: Thomas Marent / Visuals Unlimited (br). 13 Corbis:
David A. Northcott (tr). Dorling Kindersley: Thomas Marent (bl). Science Photo
Library: Claude Nuridsany & Marie Perennou (br); Gregory Dimijian (bc).
14 Corbis: Seth Patterson (MYN) / Nature Picture Library (c, br). 15 123RF.com:
somkku9kanokwan (t). Corbis: Jack Goldfarb / Design Pics (bc, br). Science
Photo Library: Suzanne L. Collins (bl). 16 Alamy Images: Thomas Kitchin &
Victoria Hurst / Design Pics Inc. (tl). Dreamstime.com: Anna Bakulina (br).
17 Dreamstime.com: Mgkuijpers (bc). 18–19 Corbis: Jochen Lübke / dpa (c).
19 Corbis: Digital Zoo (br). 20–21 Corbis: DLILLC (c). 20 Corbis: Michael &
Patricia Fogden (clb). Dreamstime.com: Amwu (br). 22–23 Corbis: David A.
Northcott (c). 22 Dreamstime.com: Isselee (br). 23 Corbis: Adam Jones / Visuals
Unlimited (br). Dorling Kindersley: Jerry Young (bc). 24 Corbis: Kennan Ward (c).
Science Photo Library: Dr. Morley Read (br). 25 Alamy Images: Amazon-Images (t).
26–27 Alamy Images: Alex Haas / Image Quest Marine (br). 26 Alamy Images:
blickwinkel (br). Getty Images: Betty & Dr. Nathan Cohen / Visuals Unlimited,
Inc. (cla). 27 Alamy Images: blickwinkel (bc). 28 Corbis: Michael & Patricia
Fogden (c). Dorling Kindersley: Jerry Young (br). 29 Alamy Images: Life on
white (bc). Dorling Kindersley: Jerry Young (bl); Thomas Marent (t).
30 Getty Images: American Images Inc (b). 31 Corbis: Fritz Rauschenbach (fbr);
Joe McDonald (tr); Michael Durham / Minden Pictures (clb); Stephen Dalton /
Minden Pictures (br). Dorling Kindersley: Jerry Young (cr). Dreamstime.com:
Lorna (tl); Regien Paassen (bl). Getty Images: American Images Inc (cra, cl).
32 123RF.com: somkku9kanokwan (tl). Alamy Images: Alex Haas / Image Quest
Marine (cla). Corbis: David A. Northcott (clb).
Dorling Kindersley: Thomas Marent (cl)
Jacket: Corbis: Paul Souders.

All other images © Dorling Kindersley Limited
For further information see: www.dkimages.com

A WORLD OF IDEAS:
**SEE ALL THERE IS TO KNOW**
**www.dk.com**

# Contents

**DK READERS**

LEARNING
pre-level
1
TO READ

# Frogs and Toads

Croak!
The frogs and
toads have come
to see you!

Common frogs live
near ponds and
in tall grass.

eye    pond

common frogs

grass

Common toads
have no teeth.
They have very
long tongues.

common toads

mouth

tongue

eardrum

bullfrogs

# Bullfrogs make very deep sounds like bulls.

eye

CROAK!

Mantellas can be
many colors—
black, blue, orange,
yellow, or green.

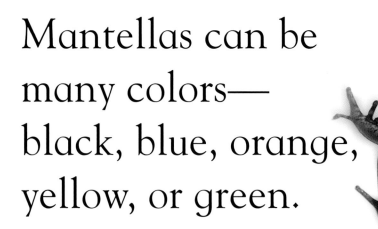

orange

mantellas

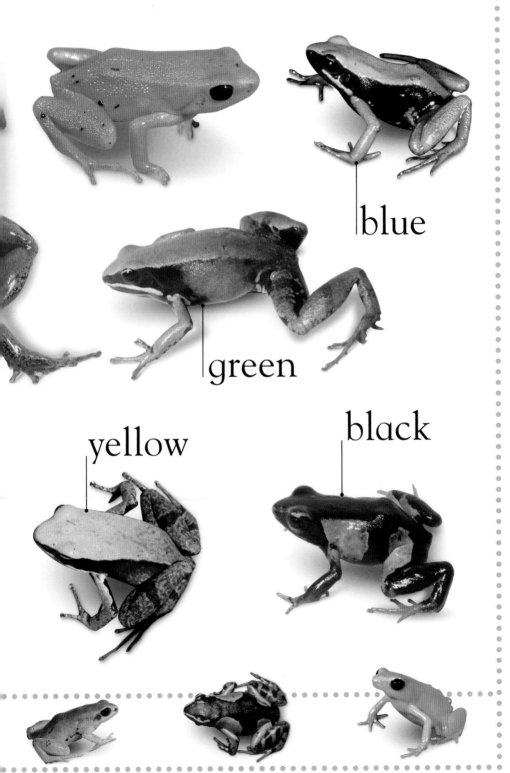

blue

green

yellow

black

13

Burrowing toads
dig holes with
their back feet.
Their back feet are
shaped like spades.

feet

burrowing toads

hole

snake

poison-dart frogs

An animal could
die if it eats
a poison-dart frog.

skin

eye

cane toads

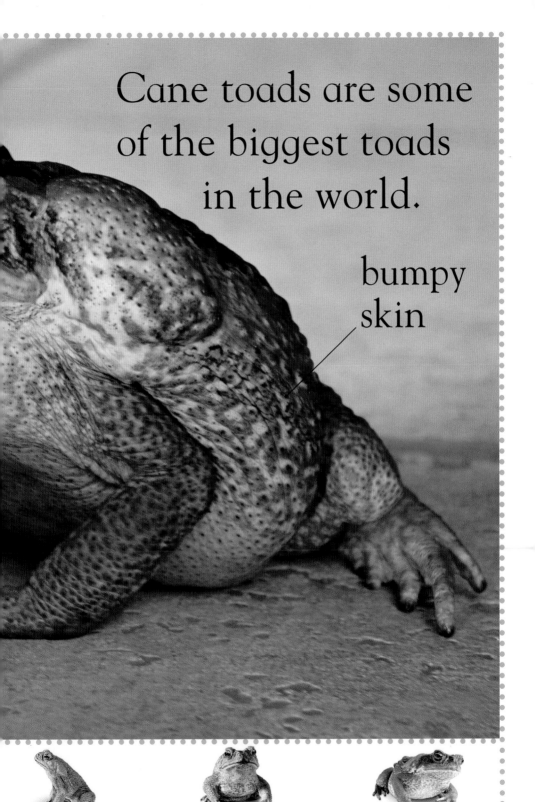

Cane toads are some
of the biggest toads
in the world.

bumpy
skin

Tree frogs can be tiny.
They live and hide
in trees.

tree
branch

tree frogs

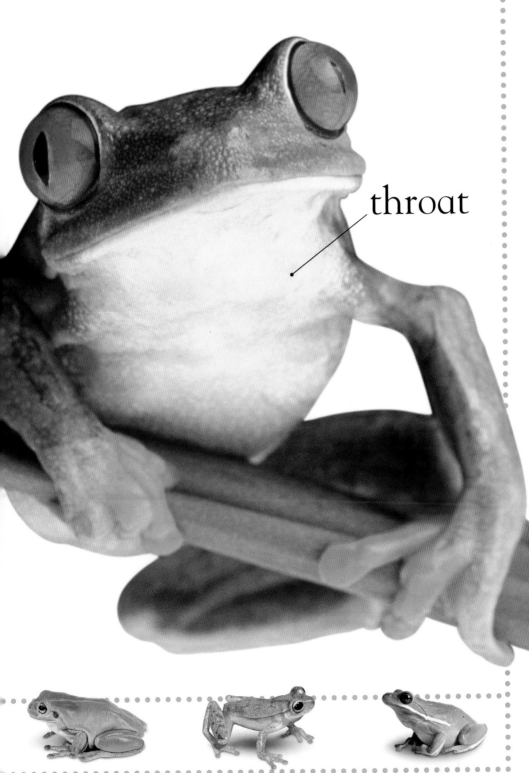

throat

Fire-bellied toads have bright bellies that scare animals away.

spots

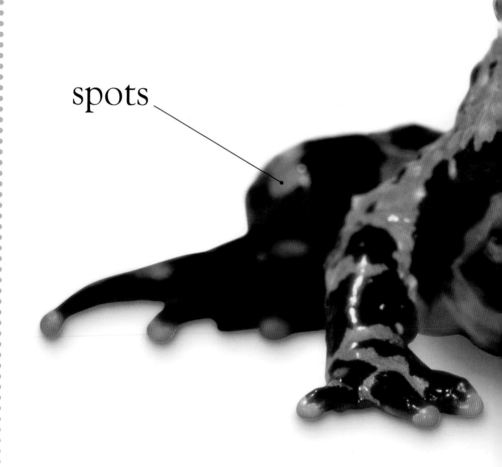

fire-bellied toads

belly

The skin of glass frogs
can be seen through,
like glass.

skin

round fingers

glass frogs

# Other frogs have round fingers.

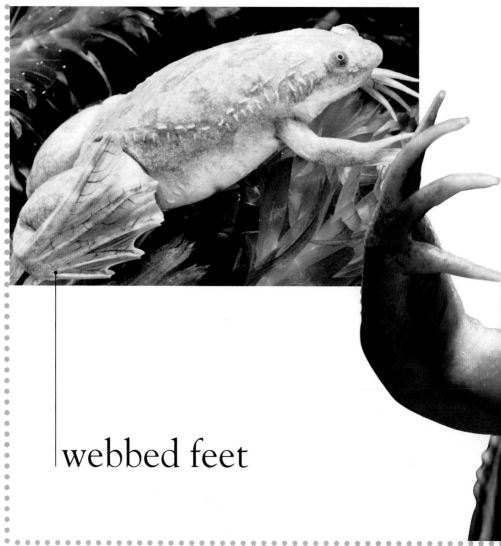

webbed feet

clawed frogs

# Clawed frogs have pointed claws.

claws

Horned frogs have horns that look like big, pointed eyebrows.

horn

horned frogs

The frogs and toads
jump away.
Off they go!
Croak!

Can you leap like a frog?

# Glossary

**Burrow**
the hole where
an animal lives

**Claw**
a pointed nail some animals
have on their fingers

**Horns**
points on an animal's head

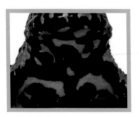
**Skin**
the covering of
an animal's body

**Tongue**
a mouth part for tasting,
eating, and making sounds